ETHICS OF POLITICS

International Relations

Nick Hunter

Heinemann
LIBRARY
Chicago, Illinois

www.capstonepub.com
Visit our website to find out
more information about
Heinemann-Raintree books.

To order:
☎ Phone 800-747-4992
🖳 Visit www.capstonepub.com
to browse our catalog and order online.

Edited by Adam Miller, Louise Galpine, and
Adrian Vigliano
Designed by Marcus Bell
Original illustrations © Capstone Global Library Ltd.
Illustrated by Darren Lingard
Picture research by Tracy Cummins
Production by Alison Parsons
Originated by Capstone Global Library Ltd.
Printed and bound in China by Leo Paper Products Ltd.

16 15 14 13 12
10 9 8 7 6 5 4 3 2 1

Library of Congress Cataloging-in-Publication Data
Hunter, Nick.
  International relations / Nick Hunter.
    p. cm.—(Ethics of politics)
  Includes bibliographical references and index.
  ISBN 978-1-4329-6549-5 (hb)—ISBN 978-1-4329-
6554-9 (pb) 1. International relations—Case studies. 2.
Diplomacy—Case studies. 3. International agencies. I.
Title.
  JZ1242.H86 2012
  327—dc23   2011043984

Acknowledgments
The author and publishers are grateful to the following
for permission to reproduce copyright material:
Corbis pp. 9 (© Reuters), 12 (© Christie's Images), 15
(© CORBIS), 21 (© epa), 25 (© Shawn Baldwin), 30
(© Nigel Pavitt/JAI), 39 (© Jiri Rezac/ Greenpeace/
Handout/dpa), 43 (© MARTIN MEISSNER POOL/
epa), 44 (© NYEIN CHAN NAING/epa), 47 (©
WISSAM HISHMI/epa), 49 (© Peter Turnley), 53 (©
Gero Breloer/epa); Getty Images pp. 10 (Ethel Davies),
19 (SIMON MAINA/AFP), 26 (SAIF DAHLAH/AFP),
28 (CHRISTOPHE SIMON/AFP), 35 (John Moore), 45
(Chris Hondros), 51 (Yawar Nazir); istockphoto p. 33
(© africa924); Shutterstock pp. 5 (© James A Dawson),
7 (© SVLuma), 16 (© Andy Lidstone), 36 (© claudio
zaccherini), 38 (© njannetti), 40 (© Photodynamic), 41
(© Frontpage).

Cover photograph of the flag of each country
reproduced with the permission of istockphoto (©
bjdlzx).

We would like to thank Jonathan Lipman for his
invaluable help in the preparation of this book.

Every effort has been made to contact copyright holders
of any material reproduced in this book. Any omissions
will be rectified in subsequent printings if notice is
given to the publisher.

CONTENTS

Some words are printed in bold, **like this**. You can find out what they mean by looking in the glossary.

POLITICS AND ETHICS

What does the word **politics** mean to you? For many people, politics brings to mind images of men and women in gray suits arguing about **taxes**, hospitals, and schools. This is one aspect of politics, but there is much more to it. The decisions made by politicians have a major impact on all our lives, from what we learn in school to the work we do and how much money we have in our pockets.

Politics can include any aspect of how people relate to each other, particularly how societies govern and set rules for themselves. This can mean setting rules for how individuals and families behave. It is also about deciding how people should pay for things that benefit the whole society, such as schools. Politics also affects how different units of society relate to each other. This includes the relationships between different countries and governments, as well as how they use their power and influence in the world. How we relate to each other on a global scale is called international relations.

Ethical questions

How these relationships work and how they are managed raise lots of questions about **ethics**, or what is right and wrong. If politics is the science of how societies are governed, then the ethics of politics is about determining the *right* way to govern and organize society. Some of the most important **ethical** questions in politics include how governments use and misuse power.

Ethical questions also involve what rights and responsibilities individuals have within society. There are many disagreements within any society about ethical questions. The right way to behave toward our fellow citizens is at the heart of divisions between **political** parties within a **democratic** society. Ethics are also an essential part of international relations. But when we try to solve ethical questions among many different countries and cultures, the divisions become even more marked.

"Those who would treat politics and morality [ideas of right and wrong] apart will never understand the one or the other."[1]

British politician John Morley, 1886

Interconnected world

When we see disagreements or conflicts between nations on the news, it is easy to think that these countries are far away and do not affect our lives. But this is not the case. The countries of the world are more interconnected than ever before. Many of the things we rely on in our lives, from food to clothes, are produced in countries on the other side of the world. Many countries are home to people who have moved from elsewhere in the world. Tensions thousands of miles away can bring conflict to our own streets.

This book will explore how international relations have developed. We will look at how ethics determine the ways in which nations behave toward one another, as well as the issues this raises. We will also look at some of the ethical and political questions facing the global community.

In 2011, Egyptians celebrated a revolution that they hoped would bring greater political freedom to their country. These events also had a major impact on many other countries in the region.

WHAT ARE INTERNATIONAL RELATIONS?

When you think about international relations, perhaps you picture leaders of different countries having meetings and signing **treaties** with one another. This is a major feature of international relations, but it is far from the whole story.

Relationships between countries are rarely as simple as one government agreeing with another. Governments may have agreements to support each other in time of conflict, even if they strongly disagree about many other issues. There may also be countries that are political and military **allies**, but that at the same time compete to sell goods and products to other countries. In addition to the direct relationships between governments, international relations are conducted by organizations that bring together countries with shared interests. Good examples are the North American Free Trade Agreement (NAFTA) or the Association of Southeast Asian Nations (ASEAN) (see pages 16 and 17). Other countries group together around specific interests, such as the Organization of Petroleum Exporting Countries (OPEC), which has members in Asia, Africa, and South America. OPEC's members are all big producers of oil.

There are also many organizations that are not made up of countries, but that are active in many parts of the world and play important roles in the international community. These organizations can have a big influence on international relations. These range from charities and groups supporting specific causes, such as the environmental group Greenpeace, to religious organizations like the Catholic Church. **Multinational corporations** with businesses in many different locations also have a major influence around the world.

Terrorists and guerrillas

Some of the global organizations that affect international relations are much less welcome for many people. These include **terrorist** groups such as al-Qaeda, which has launched attacks against the United States and its allies, but also against countries in the Islamic world that it sees as being **corrupt**. Other **guerrilla** groups can be supported by one country against another.

Examples include **militants** in the Indian-controlled region of Kashmir (see pages 50 and 51) who, according to the Indian government, receive support from neighboring Pakistan.[1]

THE UNITED NATIONS

The United Nations (UN) was created in 1945, following the two world wars. Its aim was to promote peace, solve **economic** and social problems through international cooperation, and safeguard **human rights**.

The UN now has more than 190 member countries and is led by a secretary-general, who is elected by the member countries. These countries send representatives to the UN General Assembly, which meets in New York City. Other UN bodies include the Security Council, which deals with peace and security. The Economic and Social Committee gives a global focus to these issues, while the International Court of Justice handles disputes between countries.[2] The UN does a lot of work to prevent conflict and meet its other aims. However, it is often limited by disagreements within the Security Council and other bodies.[3]

The United Nations has its headquarters in New York City.

Approaches to international relations

There are a number of different approaches that governments or other organizations can take in their relations with other countries and global organizations.

Use of power

Some would argue that international relations are a constant struggle for power. This theory is based on military power. Italian thinker Niccolo Machiavelli's *The Prince*, one of the most influential texts on government, set forward these ideas. According to this theory, countries only achieve what they want by demonstrating their power. Those that do not or cannot show strength will lose out in the international struggle, or they will need to build **alliances** that give them the necessary levels of security.

This negative view of international relations has been seen in history—for example, in the period known as the **Cold War** (see pages 15 and 16). The Cold War alliances that built up between the United States and its allies and between the **Soviet Union** and its allies were based on these ideas.

NICCOLO MACHIAVELLI (1469–1527)

Machiavelli was a statesman in the republic of Florence, in what is now Italy. He used his experience in government to write one of the most influential political books in history, *The Prince* (1513). This was a handbook for gaining and using power. Machiavelli argued that, in order for a prince to gain power and lead a **state**, it was important to be strong. He argued that this might mean lying or using unethical means.[4]

A connected world

An alternative theory is that different people around the world are interconnected. This theory emphasizes the many things that people share, ranging from natural resources like oil and water to the interconnected global **economy**. For example, multinational corporations often have more wealth and power than many countries, and they operate in many different areas. Followers of this idea of an interconnected world would argue that this interdependence helps to create peace and prosperity for all.[5]

In 1989, many **communist** governments in Europe were toppled by popular protests. This marked the end of the Cold War. Many people hoped this would lead to more cooperation among countries. But military power still remains a central part of international relations today.

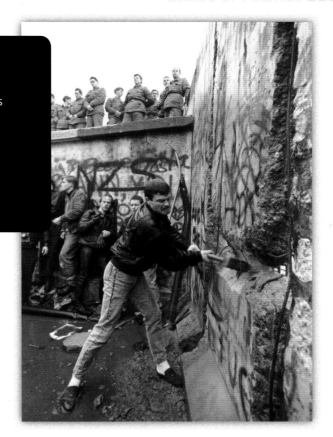

The real world

Most countries and organizations steer a course somewhere between these opposing theories. The United States is the biggest military power in the world and has the ability to enforce its will through military force, similar to what is described in Machiavelli's theories. However, like all countries, it needs to build alliances. The United States also needs to buy and sell goods around the world. So, it cannot simply be aggressive all the time. Instead, it must keep up good relations with much of the world.

At the same time, the idea of a world based solely on peace and prosperity through interconnectedness is very different from the world that exists. At any time, there are many wars and conflicts going on around the world. Many of the world's biggest issues, such as environmental change, are not tackled by the world as a whole because they do not reflect the immediate interests of some individual countries (see pages 38 and 39).

This book will look at how the international community deals with these issues, as well as the ethical questions that arise. But first we need to understand how today's complex system of international relations has developed.

FROM INDIVIDUAL STATES TO GLOBAL ORGANIZATIONS

In ancient times, the world was not rigidly divided into countries as it is now. The first individual states that dealt regularly with each other were the many states of ancient Greece. City-states such as Athens and Sparta often fought against each other, but they also recognized that they shared many aspects of language and culture. They would work together to fight off invaders such as the Persians.

Different groups or tribes of people came together in **empires**, in which rulers conquered the land around them. The biggest and most enduring of these was the Roman Empire, which ruled much of Europe and the lands around the Mediterranean Sea for almost 1,000 years. The Romans did not really recognize other countries. Rather, they regarded them simply as places they had not yet conquered.[1]

The Roman Empire united many different people and cultures. These ranged from the Middle East to Hadrian's Wall in northern Great Britain. This photo shows Roman gravestones taken from a site in North Africa.

After the fall of the Roman Empire in 476 CE, divisions between states became even less clear. Rulers often invaded each other's land. The Catholic Church gradually helped unify Europe. Meanwhile, Islam spread through the former Roman territories in the Middle East and North Africa from the 7th century.

THE CATHOLIC CHURCH

Religion played an important role in establishing the system of states. Although Europeans spoke many different languages, they all came to share the same religion. At least until the Reformation, the Catholic Church and the pope in Rome had a huge amount of power over Christianity. The Church and the Christian faith provided the ethical basis for international law. Sharing a common religion meant that states were more likely to deal with each other fairly in peace and war, and the Church was a higher authority. That does not mean that the influence of religion on international relations has always been good, however. Religion has been used as the justification for some of humanity's greatest crimes.

States, nations, and exploration

In the early 16th century in Europe, a split between Catholic and Protestant churches, called the Reformation, led to a period of conflict between states and rulers. This reached its height during the Thirty Years' War (1618–1648). The Peace of Westphalia, which ended the war, is often seen as the birth of the modern state. It established the rights of smaller countries to govern themselves, form alliances, and follow the religion their ruler chose.[2]

After 1648, the independent state was the normal form of political organization in Europe. In some cases, states shared a common culture—but not always. In areas outside Europe, such as Africa, the idea of the state was not established widely. But some states were established based on clear geographical or cultural boundaries. For example, this was the case with the island nation of Japan, in East Asia.

From the late 1400s, Europeans began exploring the world. This made international relations even more important. When Europeans met established civilizations in Asia, such as China and Japan, trading relationships required the building of trust—and the offer of benefits—with these trading partners. At the same time, in many parts of the world Europeans treated the indigenous (native) peoples as sources of gold and often slave labor.

The growth of European empires

As European nations grew more powerful, they looked to build empires of their own in the lands they had discovered outside Europe. In the centuries that followed, voyages by explorers such as Christopher Columbus, saw Europeans establish **colonies** on all other continents.

Previous leaders had created empires by conquering nearby lands. This was the case with the Romans and the Mongol Empire in Asia. But the new empires were established far away and involved dividing up continents into different countries or areas of influence. The Americas were the first region where Europeans developed colonies, with Spain and Portugal controlling most of Central America and South America. There were 13 British colonies on the east coast of North America, along with Spanish and French colonies elsewhere in what was to become the United States of America.

SIMON BOLIVAR (1783–1830)

Simon Bolivar was known as "the Liberator" for his role in freeing several South American nations from Spanish rule, including Venezuela, Colombia, Peru, Bolivia, and Ecuador. Bolivar came from a wealthy family in Venezuela, but he spent much of his childhood in Europe. In 1811, Bolivar led a revolution in his home country and other countries in the region. Afterward, Bolivar remained actively involved in the politics of these states.[3]

There were many ethical questions at the heart of the European empires—and these questions are still influencing international relations today. Many countries did not extend the same rights to citizens of their colonies as they did to those who lived in the home country. The idea that North American colonists had to pay taxes but were not represented in the Parliament that passed laws on taxes was a major cause of the American Revolution. This revolution eventually ended British rule in 1783.

This map shows the extent of European empires in 1914.

Russian Empire

Ottoman Empire

N
W — E
S

- Belgium
- France
- German Empire
- Great Britain
- Italy
- The Netherlands
- Portugal
- Spain
- United States
- Other independent States

Racism was also a feature of the age of empires, and sometimes resulted in the enslavement of non-Europeans. However, even in more enlightened empires, government by the white elite reflected the view that native peoples could not govern themselves without the guidance of Europeans.

Although all empires had faults, it can be argued that there were some benefits. Supporters argue that **democracy**, the current system of government in most countries, was spread around the world by British **colonization**. Places like Australia, Canada, and the United States provided the chance of a new life for many who had been poor in Europe. Despite these benefits, it is now widely accepted that different countries should rule themselves, rather than becoming colonies of another country.

The following quotes demonstrate two opposing views of empire:

"Exploit the resources of an India, a Burma...take all the wealth out of those countries, but never put anything back. All you're doing is storing up the kind of trouble that leads to war."[4]

former U.S. President Franklin D. Roosevelt (served 1933–1945)

"English supremacy should last until the end of time, because it means universal freedom, universal liberty, emancipation [freedom] from everything degrading."[5]

former Canadian Prime Minister Alexander Mackenzie (served 1873–1878)

World wars

At the beginning of the 20th century, European empires were at their height. The United Kingdom, France, and Germany started to come into conflict over their colonies and influence in Africa. At the same time, the Turkish Ottoman Empire, which had controlled a large empire from Southern Europe to North Africa and the Middle East, began to fall apart. This led to many new nations fighting for their independence.

All of these developments led to tensions within and among the world's major empires. These were one of the causes of World War I, which raged across Europe and other parts of the world between 1914 and 1918. Previous wars had usually been fought between professional armies. This was the first global "total war" in which the entire industry and people of the warring nations were set in motion to win the war. More than 15 million **civilians** and soldiers lost their lives in World War I, and many millions more were injured.[6] It was the most destructive conflict that humanity had known.

Lasting peace?

When World War I finally came to an end, the victorious nations met in Paris, France, to agree upon a peace settlement. The defeated countries were not invited. The United Kingdom and especially France wanted to punish Germany and its allies, which they believed had caused the war. The Treaty of Versailles blamed Germany and required its people to cover the cost of the war by paying reparations, which are payments made to make amends for something.[7] The treaty also created a League of Nations to help resolve future disputes.

But this league was not given enough power to prevent aggression by Germany, Japan, and Italy in the 1930s. The peace settlement was used by Adolf Hitler to convince Germans that their country had been unfairly treated after World War I. Many people believe the settlement was a major cause of World War II.

Just over 20 years later, the world was once again at war. World War II (1939–1945) was fought on almost every continent, and as many as 60 million lives were lost.[8] For the first time, most of the victims were civilians, including an estimated 6 million Jews murdered in the **genocide** of the Holocaust. The war also saw the birth of new and terrible weapons—atomic bombs, or **nuclear weapons**.

The United States unleashed atomic bombs on the Japanese cities of Hiroshima (pictured) and Nagasaki in August 1945, at the end of World War II. Debate still rages over whether the killing of many thousands of civilians in this manner was justified. It certainly brought the war to a swift end. Supporters of the use of these bombs argue that thousands more lives would have been lost if a conventional war had continued, and Japan or Germany would probably have used atomic weapons if they had been able to.

The modern world

World War II brought the age of empire to an end. The United Kingdom was shattered by the cost of victory. Former colonies such as India and many African countries gained their independence and joined the newly created United Nations.

The communist Soviet Union and the capitalist United States emerged as **superpowers**. (Communists believe the government should control all property, whereas capitalists believe people should invest money and drive the economy.) They and their allies faced each other in a tense standoff that became known as the Cold War. The Cold War had two possible outcomes: either peace or the catastrophic possibility of nuclear war.

Nations working together

In the 1980s, Soviet leader Mikhail Gorbachev began to introduce a new style of relations between the two sides in the Cold War. He also introduced reforms in the Soviet Union that led to the end of the communist era in that country and many in Eastern Europe. In some cases, new countries were formed by the collapse of communist **regimes**. This often created a new sense of crisis and conflict, as in the breakup of Yugoslavia into individual states during the 1990s.

The end of the Cold War ushered in a complex new period in international relations. The world was no longer divided into two opposing blocks of countries, and new alliances developed. Some of these were existing groups that then worked more closely together.

During the decades after World War II, Western European nations had come together in the European Economic Community (EEC). The EEC was partly an attempt to end the conflicting national interests that had led to two world wars. As the organization developed, it became the European Union (EU) in 1993. However, the recent growth of the EU to 27 nations has meant more disagreements over the speed and extent of integration (sharing government and institutions) among different member nations.

In 2002, many countries of the EU replaced their individual currencies (forms of money) with the Euro, a currency used across the EU.

Other regional organizations, such as the African Union, voice their members' interests loudly on the international stage. This gains more attention for problems than would be possible by each individual country. Some organizations focus on trade links, such as the North American Free Trade Agreement (NAFTA) between the United States, Canada, and Mexico.

A voice for smaller nations?

While these organizations may help countries in many ways, they are not always popular. Many people in Europe feel that the EU has too much power over individual countries, with many decisions being made by unelected officials. There is also potential for more powerful countries having too much influence within these groups. The Association of Southeast Asian Nations (ASEAN) includes many nations in Southeast Asia, but it does not include China and Japan. This is because of fears that these economic giants would have too much control over the organization.[9]

The remaining superpower

When the Soviet Union broke up in 1991, this left the United States as the world's only superpower.[10] The United States has the world's largest economy and the most advanced and powerful military force. The power of the United States means it is often expected to act as "the world's police force," getting involved in conflicts around the world. This power also causes resentment among those who disagree with U.S. **policies**.

THE COMMONWEALTH

The Commonwealth is made up of 53 member countries from every continent in the world. Almost all these countries were once part of the British Empire, ranging from mighty India, the world's biggest democracy, to tiny Tuvalu, an island nation in the Pacific. The Commonwealth nations have little in common apart from their shared history and values. Their goals are the promotion of democracy, the rule of law (making the law the final authority), good government, and social justice. The United Kingdom's Queen Elizabeth II is head of the Commonwealth.[11]

CONFLICT AND PEACE

One of the main responsibilities of any government is to protect its citizens. The aim of most political leaders is to make their nation safe and to achieve its goals without having to enter a conflict. This is a major focus of international relations. However, at any time there are numerous wars and small-scale conflicts going on around the world. The last century was scarred by the two world wars, which were the most destructive conflicts in human history (see pages 14 and 15).

Wars can be fought between countries or groups of allied countries. But this is not the only kind of conflict in the world. Some conflicts involve people fighting to form an independent country, as in the conflict to gain independence for the Russian region of Chechnya. In others, rebels are fighting to take over the government of the country, as happened in the North African country of Libya in 2011. Wars can be fought by armies in open battles or by guerrilla fighters trying to inflict damage on a larger force. They can also be fought by terrorists who kill and injure civilians in the hope of achieving their political goals. Many of the most urgent issues in international relations are about stopping these wars and preventing future conflict.

THE UN SECURITY COUNCIL

The Security Council is the body of the United Nations that is responsible for peace and security. There are five permanent members of the Security Council: China, France, Russia, the United Kingdom, and the United States. There are also 10 other members, elected for two-year terms.[1] The council aims to rule on international issues in order to prevent or end conflict. In extreme cases, it can recommend **sanctions** or military action against aggressive nations. On many occasions, particularly during the Cold War, the Security Council has been less effective than it should be, largely because each of the permanent members can **veto** action.[2] There have been calls for change, as the world has changed greatly since the system of permanent members was set up based on the countries on the winning side in World War II.

Why do people go to war?

People or countries decide to go to war to achieve something that they cannot achieve by normal political means. The goal has to be important to them, because wars cost money and, more importantly, the lives of soldiers and civilians. Countries may also go to war if they feel that they are under threat. Deciding to go to war is an extremely difficult decision for most political leaders. Democratic leaders need to make the case for war to the people who voted them into government.

But sometimes wars can be caused by leaders who have little concern for the welfare of their citizens. Examples of leaders who seem to fit this description, such as Nazi Germany's Adolf Hitler and Iraq's Saddam Hussein, are rare. Even these war leaders need to gain some support from the people—since the people will fight the war for them.

"War is the continuation of politics by other means."[3]

Karl von Clausewitz, Prussian military thinker, in his book *On War*

The UN Security Council can send peacekeeping forces to prevent conflict. They wear blue helmets to distinguish themselves from people directly involved in the conflict.

What is a just war?

There are many reasons why states or political leaders decide to go to war. But can going to war ever be justified? One of the ways we can decide if a war is just, or fair and right, is to ask whether things would have been worse if the war had not been fought. This can be difficult to calculate. World War II is often given as an example of a just war, because of the killing of millions of people by Nazi Germany during the Holocaust. However, the horrors of the Holocaust and other crimes could not have been predicted at the start of the war.

Is it right to defend yourself from attack but not to attack others? This is not as clear-cut as you might think. After all, an attack on someone else might be right if it prevents further bloodshed. A defensive war may not be just if it causes unnecessary violence—for example, if a whole population is attacked for the actions of a small minority.

What can I do?

Is there anything individuals can do to prevent conflict? If you disagree with your own country's policies, you can contact local or national politicians to express your views. There may also be an organized protest movement that you can join.

The rules of war

The UN Charter says that no nation should take up arms against another. The only exceptions are if the nation is acting in self-defense against an aggressive nation or group, or if the Security Council authorizes the action.[4] There are many conflicts around the world that do not fit this definition of a legal war.

There are also rules about how war should be fought. These rules are called the Geneva Conventions. The first rule, about the treatment of wounded soldiers, was passed in 1864. The Geneva Conventions cover the treatment of prisoners of war, protection of civilians, and the use of chemical and biological weapons.[5] While most countries have agreed to follow the Geneva Conventions, they have not always been observed in wartime.

Iraqi leader Saddam Hussein was removed from power in 2003. He was executed in 2006 after being convicted by an Iraqi court for crimes against humanity.

War in Iraq

Many questions have been asked about the decision of the U.S. and UK governments to invade Iraq in March 2003. Opinion is still divided on whether or not the war was legal. The UN Security Council did not authorize the war. The U.S. and UK leaders claimed that the war was justified as **preemptive** self-defense against Iraq's **weapons of mass destruction**, which could be used to attack other countries.[6] However, this differs from the UN definition of self-defense.[7] Also, these weapons were never found, and UN weapons inspectors said they had not been allowed sufficient time to find them before the conflict started. The website www.iraqbodycount.org estimates that more than 100,000 people have died as a result of the war and the unrest that followed.[8]

"I can apologize for the information that turned out to be wrong [regarding weapons of mass destruction], but I can't, sincerely at least, apologize for removing Saddam."[9]

former British prime minister Tony Blair, speaking in 2004

Weapons of mass destruction

Since the Cold War, people have lived with the idea that the United States and Russia, formerly the Soviet Union, have enough nuclear weapons to wipe out everyone on Earth. The delicate peace of the Cold War was based on the idea of "mutually assured destruction." Both sides knew that any nuclear attack on their enemy would inevitably lead to their own destruction, as early warning systems would allow the enemy to launch its own nuclear strike.

The post–Cold War world is much more complex, with at least eight nuclear powers (see map at right). Iran and North Korea either have nuclear weapons or are very close to developing them, and many other countries have the technology to develop nuclear weapons.

North Korea

In 2006, the secretive communist country of North Korea announced that it had tested a nuclear bomb. In 2007, North Korea agreed to close down its nuclear program in exchange for aid from other countries, but this was only temporary. North Korea pulled out of negotiations with the International Atomic Energy Agency (IAEA) in 2009 and staged another nuclear test. These developments coincided with increased tensions between North and South Korea. In addition to the threat posed by North Korea to its neighbors, North Korea has also put nuclear developments ahead of the welfare of its people, many of whom do not even have enough to eat.[10]

The Nuclear Non-Proliferation Treaty came into force in 1970. It was intended to restrict the spread of nuclear weapons to new countries and to prevent existing nuclear powers from developing new and more powerful weapons. The treaty favored those countries that already possessed nuclear weapons. Also, powerful countries continued to develop new weapons—in defiance of the treaty.[11] Countries that do not have nuclear weapons would argue that they have a right to the protection that nuclear weapons provide, and that larger nations are trying to maintain their own power by cracking down on the spread of nuclear weapons.

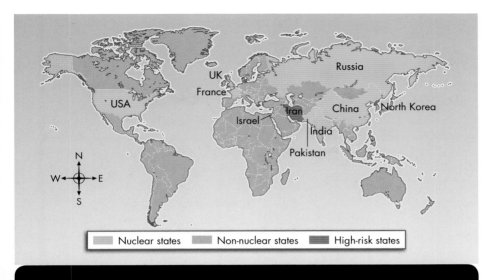

There are currently eight known nuclear powers in the world.[12] The more countries that have nuclear weapons, the greater the risk of a nuclear explosion—whether by accident or on purpose.

INTERNATIONAL ATOMIC ENERGY AGENCY

The International Atomic Energy Agency (IAEA) was set up in 1957 to promote the peaceful use of nuclear energy. It sets up and monitors safety standards for nuclear energy around the world. The organization ensures that information about nuclear accidents, such as the 2011 accident at Fukushima, Japan, is correct and available to the international community. The IAEA also has an important role in checking that countries are not developing nuclear weapons under the cover of nuclear power installations.[13] In 2005, the Nobel Peace Prize was awarded to the IAEA and its director, General Mohamed el-Baradei.[14]

Chemical and biological weapons

Chemical and biological weapons are cheaper and easier to produce than nuclear arms, but they can still have horrific effects. This was shown in 1988, when Iraq's Saddam Hussein used chemical weapons against Kurds in the Iraqi town of Halabja, killing around 5,000 people. There are international agreements banning these weapons. Still, there are concerns that inspections do not have enough political backing from powerful countries, as shown by the way inspectors were treated in the run-up to the invasion of Iraq in 2003.

Intervening in conflict

Many of the conflicts going on around the world do not capture the interest of **Western** media such as newspapers and television news. These conflicts are rarely featured in the news, but they affect the lives of millions of people in many countries. Why does the international community not get involved to end all conflicts?

In 2011, there were 15 UN peacekeeping missions around the world, from Kosovo in Southern Europe to Timor-Leste in Southeast Asia. These missions included troops from more than 100 countries around the world.[15] As the name suggests, the role of these forces is to keep peace and protect civilians, rather than to become directly involved in conflict. Peacekeeping operations do not take a side in a conflict and do not become involved—unless they or the people they are protecting are directly threatened.[16]

As we have seen, military action is only legal in self-defense or if authorized by the UN Security Council (see page 20). However, sometimes there is wide agreement that military force is needed, but the UN fails to act because of divisions on the Security Council.

Dangers of intervention

Even if it might seem that help from the outside would be a good thing, getting involved may have unforeseen and harmful consequences. If countries were allowed to **intervene** whenever they chose, this would set a dangerous example. Countries could attack each other, claiming that they were intervening to help people in that country. This has often been a tactic in the past for aggressive nations such as Nazi Germany.

Even if motives are pure, there is no guarantee that people in the affected country will see them that way. For example, some people in the Middle East are often suspicious of U.S. and European involvement in their affairs. They believe the West, especially the United States, is biased toward (favors) the interests of Israel, which often conflict with the interests of Israel's **Arab** neighbors (see pages 26 and 27).

The countries intervening might also be accused of having their own motives, such as to gain control of oil or other valuable natural resources, even if this is not the case. Concerns about countries gaining influence in sensitive areas could upset the balance of power around the world and lead to wider conflict.

UN intervention in Libya

In early 2011, a wave of protests swept across North Africa. As governments were overthrown in Tunisia and Egypt, protests started against the Libyan government of Colonel Muammar el-Qaddafi. Qaddafi's forces attacked the protestors with tanks and aircraft. In March 2011, the UN Security Council authorized an international force—including aircraft from France, the United Kingdom, and the United States—to attack Qaddafi's forces, in order to protect civilians.

While international forces were bombing Libya, the Syrian government was also using violence against its protestors, but there was no international action. Syria's government was an important ally of many countries within the region and around the world. In this case, the international community decided that the existing regime was preferable to an uncertain future, even if that regime was attacking its own people.

With help from the international community, Libya's rebels were able to defeat Qaddafi's government and take power in Libya.

The Arab–Israeli conflict

The Arab-Israeli conflict has dominated Middle Eastern affairs since the end of World War II. It is one of the most difficult problems faced by the international community. The conflict is inflamed by the fact that it concerns land that is sacred to three of the world's great religions: Islam, Judaism, and Christianity. The conflict's roots date back to the late 19th century, when Jewish settlers began to settle in Palestine. The land had been central to Judaism for thousands of years, but it was also the home of Palestinian Arabs. In 1947, the UN divided Palestine into Jewish and Arab states.

Israel declared independence in 1948, and the first of a series of wars followed between Israel, Palestinians, and neighboring Arab states such as Syria, Jordan, and Egypt. Tension continued and, in 1967, Israel launched a successful preemptive strike against its Arab neighbors. As a result, it seized land including the West Bank and East Jerusalem, both from Jordan. Since 1967, Israel has struggled for its survival against its neighbors and the forces of the Palestinian people who lost their homes after new borders were drawn.

Israel feels it has no choice, as many Arab nations—including the region's biggest power, Iran—deny its right to exist. Western, and particularly U.S., support for Israel has also damaged relations between the West and Arab countries within the region. At the same time, Palestinians feel that they have made many concessions in their search for a homeland. Terrorist attacks on Israel have had the effect of hardening positions between the two sides.

The Arab-Israeli conflict has involved attacks from both Israel and the Palestinians that have been condemned by the international community.

Obstacles to progress in the Arab–Israeli conflict[17]

Problem	Israeli view	Palestinian view
Borders: Both sides agree that there should be a separate Palestinian state. But they disagree about the borders of that state.	Israel does not want to give up all the territory it gained in 1967, including parts of Jerusalem and Israeli settlements on the West Bank.	Palestinians believe that any talks about a Palestinian state must be based on Israel's borders before it occupied territories on the West Bank in 1967.
Security: The destruction of Israel has been the aim of many militants in the Arab world. Israel is concerned that a separate Palestinian state will continue this.	Israel insists that certain factions, such as Hamas, not be allowed to control a new Palestinian state to ensure that this state is not used to attack Israel.	Palestinians believe that the only way to ensure peace is a separate Palestinian state that is free to choose its own leadership.
Refugees: Many Palestinians lived in **refugee** camps following the wars of 1948 and 1967. The UN has called for a "just settlement."[18]	Israel does not recognize any right of Palestinian refugees to return to their homes.	Palestinians insist on refugees' right to return to their homes, but some Palestinians might accept compensation (payment) for property lost by refugees.
Settlements: Israeli settlers have built homes in many areas of the territories occupied in 1967.	Israel will not give up settlements in East Jerusalem and the West Bank.	Palestinians say that settlements should be abandoned, or other land should be given as compensation.
Jerusalem: Before 1967, East Jerusalem was part of Jordan. The whole city is now controlled by Israel.	Israel sees a united Jerusalem as the capital of its country.	Palestinians want East Jerusalem as their capital. The city also contains some of Islam's holiest sites.

The Arab–Israeli conflict shows the difficulty of reaching compromise from very strongly held positions. It is possible to argue that many of the issues could be resolved. Yet the many years of resentment on both sides means that there is very little trust and room for compromise. Religious **extremists** make this worse on both sides. This became tragically evident when Israeli Prime Minister Yitzhak Rabin, who had been a major force in reaching a peace agreement, was murdered by a Jewish extremist in 1995.

Global terrorism

The worldwide tensions arising from the Arab–Israeli conflict contributed to the development of another kind of global conflict. Global terrorism has been a major concern of the international community in the 21st century.

AYMAN AL-ZAWAHIRI (BORN 1951)

Trained as a doctor, Ayman al-Zawahiri became a member of the extremist group Egyptian Islamic Jihad as a young man. In 1981, members of the group assassinated the Egyptian president Anwar Sadat. Zawahiri spent three years in prison, where persistent torture turned him into a more bitter and violent extremist. After leading a violent terror campaign in Egypt during the 1990s, he moved to Afghanistan and formed an alliance with Osama bin Laden. He became bin Laden's second-in-command and played a key role in formulating al-Qaeda's ideas. Following the killing of bin Laden by U.S. forces in 2011, Ayman al-Zawahiri emerged as the leader of al-Qaeda.

Terrorist attacks on commuters in Madrid, Spain, in 2004 are thought to have influenced the outcome of the country's elections. Some voters thought that the government's support for the United States in Iraq had made Spain a target.

Since the devastating terrorist attacks on the United States on September 11, 2001, the United States has used its military might in pursuit of terrorists. Yet the yearly number of deaths caused by international terrorism has never been more than 1,000 in the years since 2001, excluding those killed in the conflicts in Iraq and Afghanistan.[19]

Terrorism is the use of violence or the threat of violence against civilians to achieve a political goal. It usually refers to violent acts by groups of terrorists, but terrorism can also be committed by states or individuals. Terrorism itself is not new. But, since 2001, the threat has changed. In the past, publicity and gaining concessions were the main goal of terrorists, and acts of terror were a way to achieve that. Today, Islamist terrorist groups linked to al-Qaeda aim to cause maximum civilian injuries and deaths with their terrorist acts. Governments fear that these terrorists could acquire and use weapons of mass destruction.

Dealing with terrorism

The fight against terrorism creates many ethical issues for governments. Terrorists do not follow any rules when planning their attacks. Yet governments have to follow the laws of their country and international law in pursuing terrorists. They also need to strike a balance between passing laws that will prevent terrorist acts and catch terrorists, while not restricting the rights of ordinary people. There have been allegations that terrorist suspects have been denied the rights that common criminals or prisoners of war would expect during the "war on terror" fought by the United States and its allies since 2001 (see page 45).

Under suspicion

You may think that it is less important how we catch and punish terrorists, as long as it achieves the result of preventing more terrorist attacks. However, many of the laws that have been passed to make it easier to catch terrorists affect all of us. Laws have been passed to increase surveillance of (listening in on or watching) telephone calls, e-mails, and even what terrorist suspects have borrowed from libraries. Do you think this loss of privacy is a price worth paying to keep us safer?

RICH AND POOR

One of the results of trends such as **industrialization** and **imperialism** is that not all countries have developed equally. According to the World Bank, around 2.5 billion people around the world live on less than $2 per day.[1] People often speak of a divide between the countries of the rich North, such as North America and Europe, and the poor South, particularly Africa and South Asia.

An unequal world

The world's countries can be divided into **developed countries** (also called advanced industrial countries) and **developing countries** (also called less developed countries and newly industrializing countries). Newly industrializing countries such as China and South Korea have made the biggest strides in ending poverty. This has happened because these countries have developed industries that can sell goods around the world. These countries have also received investment from developed countries.

But these changes have not helped the world's least developed countries, particularly in Africa. The world's poorest countries have little opportunity to export (send away) goods to developed countries. This is, at least in part, because many countries have tariffs (taxes) and quotas, or limits, on the total number of goods brought in from overseas. Developed countries do this to protect their own farmers.

Farmers in Africa receive only a tiny fraction of the money customers pay for tea in developed countries.

The growth in global trade and communication adds to the problem. Multinational corporations can make goods in countries where they can pay workers less. But much of the money for these goods remains in the developed country where the company is based.

The problem of global poverty raises many questions about how individual governments should behave. Governments are likely to act in the interests of their own people. If they do not, people will vote out an elected government. However, many people believe that a fairer world would make it easier for the international community to tackle other issues. Making the world fairer would also be the right thing to do.

Sources of aid

The World Bank and the International Monetary Fund are linked to the United Nations and funded by the world's governments. They can provide money for development. However, this money can often come with conditions that, many people believe, make it more difficult for the countries receiving aid to develop. These conditions can include opening the countries up to international competition.

One of the biggest obstacles to progress in developing countries is the repayment of debts to richer countries. In 2005, the world's richest countries agreed to cancel the debts of many of the world's poorest countries.[2] Although this made a big difference to many people, it was not a solution that brought an end to world poverty.

WORLD TRADE ORGANIZATION

The World Trade Organization (WTO), with more than 150 member countries, provides a way for countries to debate issues about trade. It also makes the rules that govern world trade, which are primarily aimed at removing barriers so that countries and businesses can sell their goods worldwide.[3] The WTO can impose sanctions on countries that do not follow its rules.

Critics say that the WTO favors big businesses and the most powerful countries. They argue that free trade as regulated by the WTO has made rich countries richer and has not helped the poorest countries, which have far fewer resources to sell around the world.[4]

Developing nations and aid

In a more equal world, countries would be able to trade their way out of poverty. As it is, imbalances between rich and poor mean that aid, rather than trade, is a powerful tool. It can be used to lift people out of extreme poverty and to deal with crises such as floods and famines (periods without food).
In addition to acting quickly to deal with disasters, charities and nongovernmental organizations (NGOs) such as the United Nations Children's Fund (UNICEF) and Oxfam can also provide money to deal with long-term and future problems. The growing populations of the world's poorest countries are more likely to be affected by conflict than those in richer countries. The spread of **HIV/AIDS** in Africa is another issue, as it means a large number of the adult population can no longer support their families. This also puts pressure on overstretched medical resources.

UNICEF

UNICEF was set up by the United Nations after World War II to provide food and health care for children in war-torn Europe.[5] The organization's role soon broadened to protecting children around the world and upholding the UN Convention on the Rights of the Child. UNICEF works in almost 200 countries on projects related to protecting children from conflict and abuse and promoting health, nutrition, and education. In 2005, UNICEF launched a specific campaign to help the 2.5 million children living with HIV/AIDS, most of them in Africa.[6]

Aid organizations are often in a better position than individual countries to provide assistance. This is because they are trusted in a way that other countries may not be. On many occasions, countries in need of help welcome aid agencies when they are overwhelmed by a huge natural disaster. However, sometimes aid agencies have to get involved in a situation where they are not welcomed by all sides, such as when a disaster hits a country that is divided by conflict.

Long-term assistance

It can be difficult for aid agencies to strike a balance between the short-term relief of suffering—by providing food or medical care—and longer-term development projects. The best aid projects provide equipment and education that will enable the least developed countries to reduce their reliance on aid. However, if the need for aid is to be removed completely, many of the imbalances in the international system will need to be addressed.

Fighting poverty

Individuals can make a difference in helping to solve the problem of world poverty. We can all donate or raise money for charity. But we can also make changes in our lives that will help to make the world a bit fairer. Companies making everything from sportswear to consumer electronics have often, possibly unknowingly, used factories in the developing world where workers were treated badly and paid poorly. You can find out more about companies' ethical policies before you buy. Fair trade goods come with a guarantee that producers of goods such as coffee, tea, chocolate, and bananas have been paid a fair price for their products. These products may cost a bit more in your local supermarket, but choosing them will help to lift communities out of poverty.

This school was set up by an international aid organization for victims of conflict in Mozambique in southern Africa. Education will hopefully help these children to lift themselves and their communities out of poverty.

Migration

One way that people can escape poverty is by moving and working somewhere else in the world. This is called **migration**. There are currently more than 200 million people around the world living outside the country in which they were born.[7] Some of these people are refugees, fleeing war or **persecution**. But the vast majority are people who have moved to another country so they or a family member can find work. A Mexican factory worker can earn about four times as much doing the same job in the United States as he or she can earn at home.[8]

Crossing the border

The border between the United States and Mexico is the longest land border between a developed country and a developing country. Millions of people cross this border to work in the United States every year. Some are legal immigrants, but there are also an estimated 11 million illegal Mexican immigrants living in the United States. There have been many calls to crack down on the numbers of immigrants crossing the border, and security is tight at popular crossing points. However, as long as workers believe they will have a better life in the United States, they will continue to take risks crossing the desert or the Rio Grande River to reach their goal.

Immigration, which is when people move into a new country, causes a great deal of tension within international relations. People are free to move around their own country, but there are normally restrictions on moving from one country to another. Immigrants often face hostility from those already living in the country, who feel that immigrants will work for less money and take jobs from native people. Many people also feel that immigrants from overseas will change the culture of the country.

While politicians need to listen to public opinion, they also need to be aware of the benefits that immigration can bring. Immigrants can often bring much-needed skills that are in short supply. Some immigrant workers can fill jobs that native people are unwilling to do. Immigrants also create jobs by using stores and schools, and they help to pay for services by paying taxes. Immigration has helped form the culture of countries like the United States, Australia, and the United Kingdom.

Illegal immigrants from Mexico often have to walk for many days across inhospitable desert. Many people do not survive the journey.

Migration can even benefit the countries that immigrants leave, since they often send money back to families in their native country. They may also learn valuable skills and bring these skills back to their native country.

A balanced view?

Despite the many benefits of immigration, immigrants are often treated less well than native people. They are unfairly blamed when times are tough, and news reports often focus on negative stories of immigrants claiming welfare benefits. At the same time, people's lives can change dramatically when the place where they live becomes home to a large immigrant population, and it is natural that many people are uncomfortable with this.

It could be argued that immigration is one result of an unfair balance between rich and poor in the world. If people could earn money and live safely in their own countries, they would not need to take the often-hazardous journey to work in a richer country.

MANAGING OUR CROWDED PLANET

International relations are also about protecting our shared planet. Without Earth and its atmosphere, there would be no human life at all. Many of the biggest international disputes are about the extraction (removal) and use of Earth's natural resources to power modern industrial societies.

Food and water

We all need food to live. But, according to the World Bank, there are almost 1 billion people who do not have enough to eat.[1] In late 2010, food prices around the world reached an all-time high. This was partly caused by weather and other factors that affected harvests, but it was also a result of increases in demand for crops such as wheat. This demand was high because of continuing growth in the world's population.[2]

The planet's population is expected to reach 9 billion by 2050, with most growth being in Asia and Africa. This photo shows a bustling street in Hong Kong.

High food prices affect people in developing countries more than those in developed countries, as buying food takes up more of their total income. In the poorest countries, high food prices can mean the difference between eating and going hungry.[3]

Rising prices

Rising prices affect everyone. Food is our most basic need apart from water. Rising oil prices also affect everything we buy, because all goods either use oil directly when they are being made or indirectly when they are transported to stores for us to buy. Of course, oil prices also affect our own transportation costs—unless you walk or ride a bicycle!

Aid organizations point out that developed countries pay much more in subsidies (money to help stay competitive) to their own farmers than they do in food aid to developing nations.[4] Like so many areas of international relations, there is often a conflict between the interests of individual countries, which want to protect their own people, and the wider world. However, as the planet's population increases, the ethical questions about the balance between local interests and global responsibility will continue.

The thirst for oil

One reason food prices have recently risen is because some crops have been grown to make biofuels rather than food. Biofuels are substances made from plants that can be used instead of oil.

Oil is essential for many of the things we do, from powering cars to making plastics. Oil is made by a natural process over millions of years underground. It is nonrenewable, meaning it cannot be replaced once we have used it. Over time, it will become more difficult and expensive to extract (remove) oil from underground.

The countries that use the most oil are developed countries like the United States, as well as rapidly industrializing countries like China. Saudi Arabia, Iran, and other countries around the Arabian Gulf have the world's largest oil reserves. Countries that possess oil can become powerful, as other countries have to deal with them. Developed countries such as the United States that need to import oil may not question the actions of governments in oil-rich countries in the same way they would if those countries did not have oil.

Climate change

The world's obsession with oil is a major reason for one of the greatest challenges facing the international community: **climate change**. Most climate experts believe that human actions are causing the planet's climate to heat up. In particular, the **emissions** of the gas carbon dioxide (CO_2) from the burning of oil and coal is causing climate change. These experts include the Inter-Governmental Panel on Climate Change, which was formed in 1988 to provide the world's governments with information about climate change.[5] **Global warming** affects the whole world, but the impact is faster and greater in some places than others. Spreading deserts mean that droughts (lack of water) and famines in some of the world's poorest countries will become common. If climate change continues, it could seriously damage our ability to grow enough food for the planet's growing population. Melting ice in the polar regions could lead to sea level rises that will affect low-lying countries and coastal areas where millions of people live, including cities such as New York and London, England.[6]

Wind is another source of energy. Not everyone can benefit, as some parts of the world have stronger winds than others.

Despite the huge threat posed by climate change, the international community has been slow to respond. More than 190 countries have agreed to the Kyoto Protocol (1997), which promised to cut the world's CO_2 emissions by 5.2 percent from 1990 levels—with bigger cuts for developed nations. However, the U.S. president at the time, George W. Bush, withdrew from the commitments made under the protocol.[7] The targets will be very difficult to achieve if countries such as the United States and China, which recently became the world's biggest source of CO_2 emissions, cannot commit to tackling climate change.

Developed versus developing nations

In 2009, the international community came together in Copenhagen, Denmark, to try to agree on a way forward to deal with climate change. The resulting agreement recognized the scientific case for reducing climate change, but it did not lead to agreement on any commitments to cut emissions.

One of the problems is dealing with the issue of how much of a burden different countries should bear for reducing emissions. Up to now, the problem of climate change has been caused by the industrialization of today's developed nations, which began in the 18th century. Developing nations that are only just beginning to enjoy the benefits of industrialization feel that developed nations should have bigger targets for reducing emissions.

Without any international agreements, many nations are taking action to tackle their own emissions. Even China, a country where emissions have increased dramatically, is now the world's biggest investor in renewable energy sources such as solar power.[8]

Nuclear power is a controversial alternative energy source, as the fuels used give off dangerous **radiation**, plus nuclear accidents can have effects in countries far away from the original accident. The IAEA monitors nuclear energy around the world, because energy policies of one government can have effects in many other countries if something goes wrong.

Greenpeace is an environmental group that was set up by activists in 1971 and is now active in many countries. The organization uses political pressure and consumer campaigns to raise awareness of issues such as climate change and to change people's behavior.[9]

Pollution

Many other environmental challenges face the international community. The world's weather systems can carry air pollution across national boundaries. In the 1980s, a hole was discovered in the atmosphere's ozone layer. This layer of gases is important to protect Earth from the Sun's harmful radiation. The hole—located over Antarctica—was caused by chemicals used in aerosol cans (like some hair sprays) and refrigerators around the world. In the Montreal Protocol of 1987, the international community agreed to stop using these chemicals.[10]

Pollution also circulates around the world in the oceans. This can either be pollution dumped by ships or things such as plastic containers or bags that have been washed or blown away from land. Outside coastal waters, the oceans do not belong to any single country. Organizations such as the International Maritime Organization (IMO) are responsible for preventing pollution. But imposing penalties on ships that pollute is not enough to deal with the huge buildup of waste in the oceans.

Biodiversity

One of the consequences of ocean pollution is the loss of species (types) of animals and plants. The combination of life-forms in different environments—called biodiversity—is what makes Earth capable of supporting human life. If species die out, this can damage fragile ecosystems (environments made up of living things). Since 1992, most of the world's countries have signed the Convention on Biological Diversity.[11] These governments are committed to maintaining biodiversity in their countries.

The international community has managed to protect one continent from oil and mineral exploration. The Madrid Protocol, signed in 1989, agreed to protect Antarctica for 50 years.

However, as we have seen, the actions of governments are not the only factor in international relations. Multinational mining or oil companies may have operations in many different countries. While many of these companies may act responsibly, it can be difficult for governments, particularly in smaller or developing countries, to control their actions. Many governments are eager to attract these businesses and the jobs they create, so rules may not always be enforced.

The next generation

Many of these environmental challenges, including problems with food supplies and other resources, are important now, but they will become much more important for future generations. In addition to considering how their actions and laws affect other countries, politicians need to consider the impact of their decisions on future generations. For example, a decision to impose high taxes on fuel now may be unpopular, but it may prompt people to reduce their use of gasoline—which could reduce emissions for the future.

Protecting the Amazon

Rain forests have been described as the lungs of the planet. This is because they help to break down the gases, called greenhouse gases, that cause climate change. The Amazon rain forest is one of the world's most precious regions, accounting for as much as half of Earth's rain forests. The area is home to around 75 percent of the world's plant species.[12] But large areas of the rain forest have been destroyed so that animals such as cattle can graze, and for other uses.

In 2011, representatives of some of the world's rain forest nations met in Brazzaville, Congo, in Central Africa, to discuss the future of rain forests. They asked for more international funding for rain forest preservation. They argued that the whole world benefits from rain forests, so the rain forest nations should not bear the cost of preserving them.[13]

HUMAN RIGHTS

It is not only during wartime that people around the world are killed and mistreated. The international community is committed to protecting the rights with which all human beings are born. These rights are detailed in the UN Declaration on Human Rights, which was approved by the UN General Assembly in 1948.

There is a lot of debate about exactly what human rights are. It is generally agreed that they must be fundamental rights that are shared by all people. Human rights also involve tolerance of a range of views and cultures. But in many cultures, religious ideals that are shared by most of the people may actually contradict fundamental human rights, such as by discriminating against other people because of their religion or lifestyle.

Genocide

The most extreme form of human rights abuse is genocide, which is defined by the United Nations as "an act of destroying, in whole or in part, a national, **ethnic**, cultural, or religious group."[1] This may happen by murdering members of a group of people, such as the millions of Jews killed during the Holocaust in World War II, or by other means, such as imposing living conditions in which the group cannot survive or preventing members of a group from having children.

The international community, through the United Nations, is committed to preventing genocide around the world. Unfortunately, the record since World War II has not been a good one. The international community failed to act in time to prevent genocides in countries such as Cambodia (1975–1978), in Southeast Asia, and Rwanda (1994), in Central and Eastern Africa. In the North African region of Darfur, in western Sudan, more than 200,000 people have been killed since 2003, and many more have been forced to leave their homes as a result of "ethnic cleansing," which is often the same thing as genocide.

Darfur shows the limits of the international community's power to deal with serious abuses of human rights within a country. China, which has extensive economic links to Sudan, was able to use its veto as a permanent member of the Security Council (see page 18) to prevent sanctions from being imposed on Sudan. Many people think the UN system needs reform if one country can block action to deal with crimes against humanity because of its own interests. China is not the only country to have used its veto in this way.

THE INTERNATIONAL CRIMINAL COURT

Since 2002, the international community has agreed to set up the International Criminal Court (ICC). The court is set up to pursue individuals accused of genocide, war crimes, and other crimes against humanity. The ICC can only rule on crimes committed in the more than 100 countries that have accepted its authority. Unfortunately, the ICC has been weakened because several countries have not accepted this authority, including China, Russia, and the United States.[2] The United States was concerned that the court would be able to prosecute U.S. soldiers or political leaders at the request of the country's opponents.[3]

In 2011, General Ratko Mladic was brought to trial before the International Criminal Tribunal for the former Yugoslavia. He was accused of leading the massacre of more than 7,500 men and boys at Srebrenica in 1995, during Bosnia-Herzegovina's bitter war of independence from Yugoslavia.[4]

Protecting human rights

Taking action to protect human rights is not just limited to organizations such as the United Nations and the International Criminal Court. Global campaigning groups work to remain at the forefront of the battle to ensure that human rights are respected.

Human rights organizations such as Amnesty International and Human Rights Watch have an important role to play in drawing attention to human rights abuses, and in influencing the public's desire to tackle those abuses. They perform a role that governments often do not want to fill, as drawing attention to human rights issues may cause tensions between different countries—especially if the country accused of abuse is a powerful nation or an important trading partner.

AUNG SAN SUU KYI (BORN 1945)

Aung San Suu Kyi has led the fight for democracy in Myanmar (also called Burma) since 1988. As a result of her campaign, she has spent more than 15 years under house arrest in her native country. Despite this, Aung San Suu Kyi has continued to call for nonviolence in response to the often-brutal treatment of protestors by Myanmar's military government. In 1991, Aung San Suu Kyi was awarded the Nobel Peace Prize for her campaign.[5] This and other international awards have brought the attention of people around the world to the situation in Myanmar. But the fact that Myanmar is still a long way from true democracy shows the limits of international pressure when dealing with a determined regime.

Campaigning for human rights

Pressure from ordinary people around the world has often been successful in highlighting and ending abuses of human rights. Human rights groups such as Amnesty International have local groups where you can work with others to campaign for human rights. To campaign for people who have been imprisoned because of the views they hold, you can write letters or e-mails to authorities on their behalf. There are many examples of prisoners who have been released because of international pressure like this.

Rights for terrorists

Debates about human rights are often not simple. Human rights apply to everyone, regardless of who they are and the views they hold. It may be that a victim of human rights abuses holds views we do not share, but freedom to express those views is usually considered to be a human right.

The case of terrorism suspects held at the U.S. base at Guantánamo Bay, in Cuba, is a good example. After the September 11, 2001 terrorist attacks on New York City and Washington, D.C., and the U.S.-led invasion of Afghanistan that followed, many suspected members of al-Qaeda were held at Guantánamo Bay. The suspects were held without trial for long periods, and they were tried in military courts rather than going through normal federal courts. There were also allegations that torture was used when interrogating, or questioning, the alleged terrorists. Although people around the world recognized that these suspects may be terrorists with goals to commit mass murder, many people were also uncomfortable that they were not granted the same rights as other suspected criminals.

CULTURE AND RELIGION

In addition to countries and NGOs such as international aid agencies, there are many other international groups and links that have a strong influence on global relations.

Many of the world's countries have only been in existence for less than a century. Some, like the countries of the former Soviet Union, have only enjoyed full independence in the past few years. Religion and cultural identity can provide much more powerful links—or sometimes, divisions—between people than national borders or governments.

Religion

The world's major religions are all older than the idea of the nation-state. Religion also played a key role in the development of state identities in Europe in the years after the Reformation in the 16th century (see page 11). Today, many countries separate church and state, and countries such as the United States, United Kingdom, and Australia are home to people of many different religions. Still, religion can have a powerful influence on world affairs.

Iran and Islamic fundamentalism

Iran is one of the most powerful countries in the Middle East, with large oil and gas reserves and a growing population of more than 75 million.[1] In 1979, a revolution in Iran created an Islamic republic, led by religious leader Ayatollah Khomeini. Since the revolution, relations between Iran and other countries have often been hostile. The West accuses Iran of supporting extremists and terrorists around the world and of funding opposition to Israel. Governments in many of Iran's neighboring countries fear that Iran will provide help to extreme religious parties that could threaten their own power.

Mahmoud Ahmedinajad is a controversial figure. As president of Iran, he has deliberately raised tensions in relations with Israel. Although Ahmedinajad is president, ultimate power in Iran lies with the country's religious leaders.

Religious groups are often a powerful force in the promotion of ethical international relations. Examples of such groups include the international group the Red Cross and Red Crescent Movement, which protects and assists victims of conflict and prisoners of war. The Red Cross movement was born of the deep religious beliefs of its founder Henri Dunant. During the Cold War, the Catholic Church was an important focus for opposition to communist regimes in countries such as Poland, where organized religion was banned.

However, religion has not always been seen as a force for good in international relations. HIV/AIDs is a huge issue in many African nations, and many people are critical of the Catholic Church's opposition to the use of condoms, which could prevent the spread of the disease. In 2007, the head of the Catholic Church in Mozambique, in southeastern Africa, even claimed that condoms made in Europe had been deliberately infected with HIV, to discourage people from using them.[2] Religion is also a factor behind many of the world's conflicts, such as the Arab–Israeli conflict and the justification of terrorist groups such as al-Qaeda.

Different religions often have different ideas about what is ethical and moral in international relations. Countries and organizations based on strong religious beliefs may see secular (nonreligious) countries as corrupt. At the same time, these non-religious people may be upset by attitudes in more religious regimes, such as the treatment of women in some Islamic countries. It can be much more difficult to reach compromise on conflicts that are a result of religious beliefs rather than political calculations.

Nationalism

Religion is often part of a group's national identity, along with other shared characteristics such as language, culture, and history. The idea that national groups should be able to rule themselves in separate countries grew in popularity during the 20th century. This was particularly true at the end of World War I, when the empires ruled by Germany, Austria, and Turkey were dismantled. However, the ideal of countries based on national and ethnic identity proved very difficult to achieve in practice, as countries often include more than one national group or sizable minorities.

A united kingdom?

The United Kingdom is an example of a country made up of several distinct nations. Wales and England were officially united in 1536 and joined with Scotland in the Act of Union in 1707. Ireland was also united with Great Britain between 1800 and 1922, and the six counties of Northern Ireland remain part of the United Kingdom.

This union raises lots of ethical questions, as the smaller nations feel they are dominated by English culture. People in England question whether they should have their own parliament, as Scotland, Wales, and Northern Ireland do. These arguments are about how much power the central government of the union should have over smaller nations. These questions are also raised in many larger unions, such as the European Union.

Nationalism, meaning strong feelings of pride for a country, is not always a good thing. Too often in the past, nationalism has spilled over into excluding certain groups or having racist attitudes to minorities in the society. Extreme political groups that are opposed to immigration or ethnic minorities will often use the word *national* in their names, such as France's Front National or the United Kingdom's British National Party.

In the worst cases, extreme nationalism can lead to attacks on other ethnic groups or even genocide. This was a horrific feature of the wars in the former Yugoslavia in the 1990s, when ethnic groups such as the Muslims of Bosnia tried to break away from the Serbs who had dominated Yugoslavia under communism.

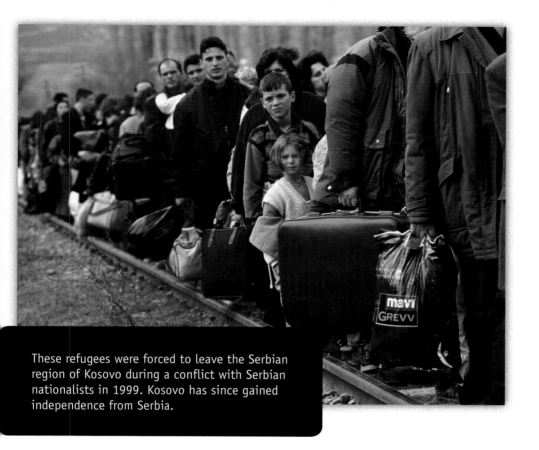

These refugees were forced to leave the Serbian region of Kosovo during a conflict with Serbian nationalists in 1999. Kosovo has since gained independence from Serbia.

Nationalism by people seeking to build their own separate states can destabilize existing ones or produce conflict. This is often the case in a state in which one ethnic group is dominant while other groups seek their independence. It can be even more complex when national groups cross more than one country, such as the Kurdish people, whose homeland crosses several countries including Turkey and Iraq, where they have faced persecution.

Respecting other groups

While it may be a good principle for national groups to have independent countries, it can also create problems—as seen in the many examples of nationalism causing conflict. There are very few countries that are made up of only one cultural group, particularly in the modern world of global migration. Nationalism can help peoples to build an identity. But it also needs to be balanced with respect for other nations and communities.

Kashmir

Kashmir is a region that lies on the border between India and Pakistan (see map below). Kashmir has been the flashpoint in relations between India and Pakistan since 1947. It is a case that shows how divisions along the lines of religion and cultural identity can create serious problems in international relations. The stakes could hardly be higher in the confrontation between these two nuclear powers.

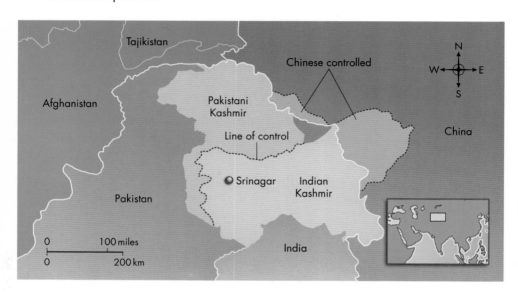

Background to a conflict

Like so many issues in international relations, the dispute over Kashmir dates back to independence from British colonial rule. In 1947, British India became two independent countries: India, where the majority of the population was Hindu, and Pakistan, where the majority was Muslim. Kashmir has a Muslim majority. Kashmir's Hindu leader wanted to remain independent, but he agreed to become part of India in exchange for military aid against attackers coming from Pakistan. India promised that the people of Kashmir would be able to vote on their future, but this never happened.[3]

Since 1947, Kashmir has been the trigger for two wars between India and Pakistan. After the first war in 1949, it was divided into Indian-controlled Kashmir and Pakistani-controlled Kashmir, which are separated by a line of control. Since 1989, militants have launched several attacks against India. Some militants want Kashmir to become part of Pakistan. Others favor independence for the region.[4]

"I told them, 'What you are doing is wrong. It will not lead you to any place other than the destruction of our state; our houses will go; our villages will be blown up; innocent people will die; many of our womenfolk will be raped and murdered.'"[5]

Farooq Abdullah, chief minister of Indian-administered Kashmir in 1989, on the Kashmiri insurgency that began that year

Search for solutions

Relations between India and Pakistan have improved over time. However, they suffered a setback when Pakistan was blamed as the source of terrorists who attacked the Indian city of Mumbai in 2008.

Any solution to the Kashmir issue would mean one or both countries having to give up territory, which they are not prepared to do. While most of the people are Muslim, there are significant minorities of Hindus and Buddhists who would not want to be part of Pakistan. The fact that India and Pakistan both have nuclear weapons has made all-out war over the region less likely, because of the fear that one or both sides might use those weapons.

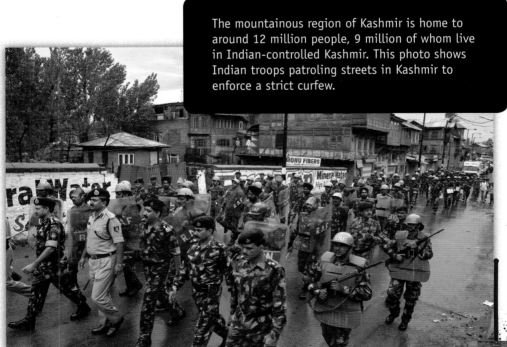

The mountainous region of Kashmir is home to around 12 million people, 9 million of whom live in Indian-controlled Kashmir. This photo shows Indian troops patroling streets in Kashmir to enforce a strict curfew.

NEW CHALLENGES AND NEW SOLUTIONS

The challenges for nations working together are varied and often very difficult to resolve. Since the mid-20th century, many of the world's flashpoints were a direct result of the Cold War and the end of communism. The end of colonial empires also created many issues, as nations struggled for independence. The legacy of colonization has also been a factor in the gap between rich and poor.

While many of these issues have still not been solved, the international community is likely to face lots of new and pressing problems in the decades to come. These include control of oil and other natural resources and continued ethnic and religious conflict. These issues will continue to raise ethical questions about how different nations relate to each other.

Population and power

The world's growing population will put new pressures on precious natural resources such as oil and land for growing food. The challenge for the global community is to resolve disputes about resources peacefully, while trying to ensure that all the world's people have enough to eat.

The balance of the world community is also changing. The economic success of countries such as China, Brazil, and India means that they will play a bigger role in international relations. Many people also believe that the Western countries that have dominated the world economy since the 20th century will become less important, as their populations grow less quickly and as they contribute less to the world economy.

FACING THE FUTURE

Many of the international issues that need to be tackled now, from conflicts to climate change, will have a much bigger impact on future generations if they are not dealt with. Young people need to be aware of the issues facing the world community so that they can help push politicians and others to make the decisions that matter for the future.

Migration is already a major strain on international relations, as people try to move to find better work opportunities, while destination countries continue trying to preserve their distinctive cultures. With the pressure on resources and improvements in travel and communications, this is likely to continue. Governments will have to decide whether the benefits of immigration outweigh the tensions immigration produces.

Threats to humanity

One of the most immediate questions that the United Nations will have to deal with is the spread of nuclear weapons and other weapons of mass destruction. There are still huge stockpiles of nuclear weapons in countries such as the United States and Russia, and the dangers will increase if more countries gain access to nuclear technology. Nuclear weapons are always at the top of any list of international issues, because a major nuclear conflict has the potential to destroy all life on Earth.

Equally serious is the threat from climate change, which could make it impossible for humans to live on our planet if it continues unchecked. Attempts to tackle global warming have so far been unsuccessful, despite widespread recognition of the dangers. This raises the question of whether international bodies such as the United Nations have enough power to really resolve the biggest concerns facing the international community. Instead, as history tells us, some of the most difficult international issues and conflicts might need to be overcome by countries working together.

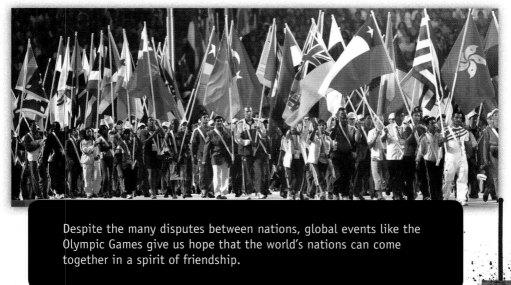

Despite the many disputes between nations, global events like the Olympic Games give us hope that the world's nations can come together in a spirit of friendship.

53

TOPICS FOR DISCUSSION

As this book shows, there are many debates about international relations and the role that ethics play in the global community.

Here are a few questions to consider:

- Take an international issue and study the roles and motivations of the different countries involved. Do you think they are acting in their own interests, or in the overall interests of the international community?

- Examine the 2011 decision by the UN to intervene in Libya to stop violence by the government there. Compare this to the UN's decision not to intervene in Syria despite similar problems. Why did the UN intervene in one country but not the other? Was this decision ethical?

- Why are there so many conflicts around the world? Do you think the United Nations is effective in preventing conflict? What would you change to make sure that conflicts could be avoided or resolved more easily?

- Examine the ongoing issues in the Sudanese region of Darfur. Various government campaigns against ethnic groups there have resulted in thousands of civilian deaths as well as many more problems. Discuss the international community's response to the issues in the region. Has enough been done to prevent violence in Darfur? What obstacles have stood in the way of effective intervention and peacekeeping?

- If you were setting up an organization like the United Nations, what would it be like? What could you do to ensure that governments would work together? What would be the most important issues to deal with?

- Should the spread of nuclear weapons be restricted? Is the world a safer place because a few nations have nuclear weapons? Do you think that countries around the world would agree to completely decommission nuclear weapons (make them no longer usable)? Examine the history of nuclear disarmament and the current debates surrounding the issue.

- Should the international community have the right to intervene in conflicts in other countries? If the United Nations cannot reach agreement on military action, should other concerned groups of countries be able to take action without going through the UN for approval? Would this make the world a safer place?

- Is war ever justified? Look at some of the conflicts going on now or in the recent past and decide if you think they are justified or not. World War II has often been called a just war. Examine this argument and decide if you agree or disagree with it.

- Can the international community do more to tackle global poverty? How would you go about ensuring that everyone has enough to eat? How does the gap between rich and poor nations affect international relations?

- Is immigration a good thing? Make a list of the benefits and drawbacks of immigration in your country. Think about why people move to your country, and also why people might leave to live in other countries.

- Is the international community doing enough to fight climate change? Should countries wait until they can agree on a global plan for dealing with climate change, or should countries take their own initiatives? Think about the arguments of developing countries, which say that action on emissions prevents them from catching up with developed countries.

- What are basic human rights? Find a copy of the UN Declaration on Human Rights (see www.un.org/en/documents/udhr/) and see if you would add any rights to this list.

GLOSSARY

alliance agreement between two countries to support each other

ally friend or supporter. Allied countries support each other in conflicts or relations with other countries.

Arab people native to countries of the Middle East and North Africa, who speak Arabic and typically follow the religion of Islam

civilian anyone who is not a member of the armed forces

climate change rise in average temperatures affecting climate on Earth

Cold War period of tension and military threats between the USA and the Soviet Union, each supported by their allies. The Cold War lasted from the end of World War II to about 1991.

colonization establishing government in another country so that it becomes part of an empire

colony country that is ruled over by another country

communist someone who believes that all property should be controlled by the government, with everyone working for the state. There were communist governments in much of Eastern Europe, the Soviet Union, and China during the second half of the 20th century.

corporation company that employs people; the term particularly refers to large businesses with branches in many countries

corrupt morally bad or fraudulent

democracy form of government in which the people of a country or region vote for the government

democratic decided by an election or vote

developed country country in which industry and the economy are fully developed. These are usually wealthier countries such as the United States and the United Kingdom.

developing country poorer country in which the economy is not yet fully developed. Examples include many countries in Africa, Asia, and South America.

economic relating to money, finance, and the world economy

economy total of all the wealth created in a society

emission greenhouse gas such as carbon dioxide created by industries and homes

empire collection of colonies ruled by another country, such as the British Empire between the 18th and 20th centuries

ethical relating to ethics and morals

ethics moral questions about the right way of doing things

ethnic with a distinctive culture

extremist anyone who holds extreme religious or political views

genocide persecution or murder of an entire people or culture

global warming widely accepted theory that Earth's climate is getting warmer because of the actions of humans, such as burning fossil fuels

guerrilla any group engaging in irregular fighting, usually against a larger force or invading army

HIV/AIDS HIV is a virus that causes AIDS, a disease that affects the immune system

human rights rights that every person has, regardless of who the person is or where he or she lives

immigration when people move from the country they were born in to the country in which they now live

imperialism process by which one country gains power over others, either by direct political control or influence

industrialization development of a society from a rural, farming economy to one based on industry and manufacturing

intervene get involved on one side or the other

migration moving from one country to another

militant extreme

multinational located or active in many different countries

nationalism strong patriotic feelings for a country, which may involve wanting independence from another country

nuclear weapon weapon that creates a huge explosion by releasing atomic energy

persecution singling out a person or group for bad treatment

policy plan that guides future decisions

political relating to politics

politics science of how societies make rules and govern themselves

preemptive action taken to prevent another event that has not yet happened, such as attacking another country to prevent that country from launching an attack

radiation particles emitted (given off) by radioactive materials—like those used in nuclear power or weapons—that are harmful to living things

refugee person who is forced to move from his or her home because of war or because of the fear of being harmed

regime government

sanction restriction imposed on a country—such as restricting what it can sell or buy—in order to force it to change its policies

Soviet Union country made up of what are now Russia, Ukraine, and several other countries. The Soviet Union opposed the United States and its allies in the Cold War. The country broke up in 1991.

state country or political division within a country

superpower country that can dominate others because of its military or economic power

tax money that is paid to the government so that it can provide public services

terrorist anyone who seeks to achieve political goals by carrying out acts of violence on civilians

treaty agreement between countries, for example to end a conflict

veto forbid or stop something

weapon of mass destruction chemical, biological, or nuclear weapon that can cause widespread death and destruction

Western referring to countries of the West, including those in North America, Western Europe, and others, that share Western economic and cultural values

NOTES ON SOURCES

Politics and Ethics (pp. 4–5)

1. Total Politics, "Quotes," http://www.totalpolitics.com/quotes/?tag=misc ellaneous&count=121.

What Are International Relations? (pp. 6–9)

1. BBC News, "Quick Guide: Kashmir Dispute," June 29, 2006, http:// news.bbc.co.uk/1/hi/world/south_asia/5030514.stm.

2. United Nations, "Main Bodies," http://www.un.org/en/mainbodies.

3. Iain McLean and Alistair McMillan, *The Concise Oxford Dictionary of Politics* (Oxford: Oxford University Press, 2009), s.v. "United Nations," http:// www.oxfordreference.com/views/ENTRY.html?subview=Main&entry=t86. e1424.

4. Margaret Drabble, ed., *Oxford Companion to English Literature*, 5th ed. (Oxford: Oxford University Press, 1995), 611.

5. Paul Wilkinson, *International Relations: A Very Short Introduction* (Oxford: Oxford University Press, 2007), 4–5.

From Individual States to Global Organizations (pp. 10–17)

1. Jenny Edkins and Maja Zehfuss, eds., *Global Politics: A New Introduction* (Abingdon, UK: Routledge, 2009), 199.

2. Wilkinson, *International Relations*, 14–15.

3. "Simón Bolívar," in *The Oxford Companion to Politics of the World*, ed. Joel Krieger (Oxford: Oxford University Press, 2001), http://www. oxfordreference.com/views/ENTRY.html?subview=Main&entry=t121.e0076.

4. Niall Ferguson, *Empire* (London: Penguin, 2004), 250.

5. The National Archives, "Living in the British Empire: The British View," http://www.nationalarchives.gov.uk/education/empire/pdf/g2cs1.pdf.

6. Norman Davies, *Europe: A History* (Oxford: Oxford University Press, 1996), 1328.

7. Davies, *Europe: A History*, 927–28.

8. *Britannica Student Encyclopedia*, s.v. "World War II," http://library. eb.co.uk/comptons/article-9277798?query=world%20war%202&ct=.

9. Wilkinson, *International Relations*, 102.

10. Angus Stevenson, ed., *Oxford Dictionary of English* (Oxford: Oxford University Press, 2010), s.v. "Soviet Union," http://www.oxfordreference. com/views/ENTRY.html?subview=Main&entry=t140.e0795100.

11. *Whitaker's Almanack 2009* (London: A&C Black, 2009), 713–14.

Conflict and Peace (pp. 18–29)

1. United Nations, "Security Council: Members," http://www.un.org/sc/members.asp.

2. Wilkinson, *International Relations*, 89–90.

3. *Oxford Dictionary of Quotations* (Oxford: Oxford University Press, 3rd edition, 1979), 152.

4. Charter of the United Nations, Chapter VII, http://www.un.org/en/documents/charter/chapter7.shtml.

5. *A Dictionary of World History* (Oxford: Oxford University Press, 2000), s.v. "Geneva Conventions," http://www.oxfordreference.com/views/ENTRY.html?subview=Main&entry=t48.e1440.

6. Wilkinson, *International Relations*, 24.

7. World Press Review, "The United Nations, International Law, and the War in Iraq," http://www.worldpress.org/specials/iraq.htm.

8. Iraq Body Count, "Documented Civilian Deaths from Violence," http://www.iraqbodycount.org.

9. Dominic Streatfield, *A History of the World Since 9/11* (London: Atlantic Books, 2011), 341.

10. BBC News, "North Korea Country Profile," February 11, 2011, http://news.bbc.co.uk/1/hi/world/asia-pacific/country_profiles/1131421.stm.

11. Wilkinson, *International Relations*, 117–18.

12. Arms Control Association, "Nuclear Weapons: Who Has What at a Glance," http://www.armscontrol.org/factsheets/Nuclearweaponswhohaswhat.

13. International Atomic Energy Agency, http://www.iaea.org.

14. Nobel Prize, "The Nobel Peace Prize 2005," http://nobelprize.org/nobel_prizes/peace/laureates/2005/#.

15. United Nations, "United Nations Peacekeeping: About Us," http://www.un.org/en/peacekeeping/about.

16. United Nations, "United Nations Peacekeeping: What Is Peacekeeping?" http://www.un.org/en/peacekeeping/operations/peacekeeping.shtml.

17. Paul Reynolds, "Middle East Peace Talks: Where They Stand," BBC News, September 27, 2011, http://www.bbc.co.uk/news/world-middle-east-11138790.

18. Don Peretz, "Arab-Israeli Conflict," in *Oxford Companion to Politics*, http://www.oxfordreference.com/views/ENTRY.html?subview=Main&entry=t121.e0035.

19. Jonathan Barker, *The No-Nonsense Guide to Global Terrorism* (Oxford: New Internationalist, 2008), 40–41.

Rich and Poor (pp. 30–35)

1. World Bank, "News and Broadcast: Poverty," http://web.worldbank. org/WBSITE/EXTERNAL/NEWS/0,,contentMDK:20040961~menuPK:3448 0~pagePK:64257043~piPK:437376~theSitePK:4607,00.html.

2. Make Poverty History, "Achievements," http://www. makepovertyhistory.org/achievements.

3. World Trade Organization, "Understanding the WTO: Basics: What Is the World Trade Organization?" http://www.wto.org/english/thewto_e/ whatis_e/tif_e/fact1_e.htm.

4. Wilkinson, *International Relations*, 133.

5. UNICEF, "About UNICEF: Who We Are," http://www.unicef.org/ about/who/index_history.html.

6. UNICEF, "What We Do," http://www.unicef.org.uk/UNICEFs-Work/ What-we-do/; UNICEF, "Child Info: Statistics by Area: HIV/AIDS," http:// www.childinfo.org/hiv_aids.html.

7. Migration Policy Institute, "MPI Data Hub: Most Populous Countries Worldwide Compared to Global Migrant Population (2010)," http://www. migrationinformation.org/DataHub/charts/worldstats_1.cfm.

8. Peter Stalker, *The No-Nonsense Guide to International Migration* (Oxford: New Internationalist, 2008), 27.

Managing Our Crowded Planet (pp. 36–41)

1. World Bank, "Food Crisis: Hunger Clock," http://www.worldbank. org/foodcrisis/.

2. Lester Brown, "The Great Food Crisis of 2011," *Foreign Policy*, January 10, 2011, http://www.foreignpolicy.com/articles/2011/01/10/the_great_ food_crisis_of_2011?page=0,3.

3. Ibid.

4. Oxfam, "Growing a Better Future," http://www.oxfam.org.uk/ resources/papers/downloads/cr-growing-better-future-170611-summ-en.pdf.

5. Intergovernmental Panel on Climate Change, "History," http://www. ipcc.ch/organization/organization_history.shtml.

6. Mark Kinver, "The ebb and flow of sea level rise," BBC News, January 22, 2008, http://news.bbc.co.uk/1/hi/sci/tech/7195752.stm.

7. Wilkinson, *International Relations*, 107–9.

8. Simon Rogers, "How China overtook the US in renewable energy," Guardian online, March 25, 2010, http://www.guardian.co.uk/news/ datablog/2010/mar/25/china-renewable-energy-pew-research.

9. Greenpeace, "About Greenpeace," http://www.greenpeace.org.uk/ about.

10. *Encyclopaedia Britannica*, s.v. "Air Pollution," http://library.eb.co.uk/eb/article-286164.

11. UN Convention on Biological Diversity, "About Biodiversity," http://www.cbd.int/2010/biodiversity/?tab=2.

12. *Britannica Student Encyclopedia*, s.v. "Amazon River," http://library.eb.co.uk/comptons/article-196244.

13. Thomas Hubert, "African Summit Calls for Action on Rainforests," BBC News, June 3, 2011, http://www.bbc.co.uk/news/world-africa-13651059.

Human Rights (pp. 42–45)
1. Wilkinson, *International Relations*, 125.

2. International Criminal Court, "The States Parties to the Rome Statute," http://www.icc-cpi.int/Menus/ASP/states+parties/.

3. Wilkinson, *International Relations*, 129.

4. BBC News, "Profile: Ratko Mladic, Bosnian Serb Army Chief," May 27, 2011, http://www.bbc.co.uk/news/world-europe-13559597.

5. Burma Campaign UK, "A Biography of Aung San Suu Kyi," http://www.burmacampaign.org.uk/index.php/burma/about-burma/about-burma/a-biography-of-aung-san-suu-kyi.

Culture and Religion (pp. 46–51)
1. BBC News, "Iran Country Profile," May 10, 2011, http://news.bbc.co.uk/1/hi/world/middle_east/country_profiles/790877.stm.

2. BBC News, "Shock at Archbishop Condom Claim," September 26, 2007, http://news.bbc.co.uk/1/hi/7014335.stm.

3. BBC News, "Q&A: Kashmir Dispute," November 6, 2008, http://news.bbc.co.uk/1/hi/world/south_asia/2739993.stm.

4. Ibid.

5. BBC News, "Kashmir Conflict 'unfinished business,'" December 8, 2009, http://news.bbc.co.uk/1/hi/world/south_asia/8400176.stm.

FIND OUT MORE

Books

Andrews, David. *Business Without Borders: Globalization* (The Global Marketplace). Chicago: Heinemann Library, 2011.

Connolly, Sean. *United Nations* (Global Organizations). Mankato, Minn.: Smart Apple Media, 2009.

Friedman, Mark. *Human Rights* (Hot Topics). Chicago: Heinemann Library, 2012.

Hynson, Colin. *New Global Economies* (World Today). Mankato, Minn.: Sea-to-Sea, 2010.

Spilsbury, Richard. *Global Economy* (Hot Topics). Chicago: Heinemann Library, 2012.

Stearman, Kaye. *Military Intervention* (Ethical Debates). New York: Rosen, 2007.

Wilkinson, Paul. *International Relations: A Very Short Introduction* (Brief Insight). New York: Sterling, 2010. (This is aimed at an adult audience but is a good introduction to the topic.)

DVDs

Dr. Strangelove (1961): Black comedy about the prospect of nuclear conflict during the Cold War.

The Gathering Storm (2002): The story of Winston Churchill and international relations in the lead-up to World War II.

The Manchurian Candidate (1962): Another story about the fear of communism during the Cold War.

Websites

Most of the organizations mentioned in this book have extensive websites detailing how they work and giving information on current issues. Here are a few examples:

www.amnesty.org/en
Amnesty International is an independent aid organization focused on ending human rights abuses around the world. Learn more at this website.

europa.eu/about-eu/index_en.htm
This website is all about the European Union (EU).

future.state.gov
The U.S. Department of State is concerned with diplomacy and international relations around the world. Find out more at this student-focused website.

www.hrw.org
Human Rights Watch in an independent aid organization dedicated to defending and protecting human rights. Find out more at this website.

www.icc-cpi.int/Menus/ICC
Learn more about the International Criminal Court at this website.

www.nato.int/cps/en/natolive/index.htm
This website explores the North Atlantic Treaty Organization (NATO).

www.un.org/en
This is the website of the United Nations (UN).

www.wto.org
This is the website of the World Trade Organization (WTO).

INDEX